Beginner's Guide
to
LACE
KNITTING

by Rita Weiss

11·23

Leisure Arts, Inc.
Maumelle, Arkansas

Produced by

Production Team

Creative Directors:	Jean Leinhauser and Rita Weiss
Technical Editor:	Mary Ann Frits
Pattern Testers:	Kimberly Britt
Knit Charts:	Susan Lowman
Book Design:	April McArthur

Diagrams © 2014 by The Creative Partners™LLC
Reproduced by special permission

We have made every effort to ensure that these instructions are accurate and complete. We cannot, however, be responsible for human error, typographical mistakes or variations in individual work.

Published by Leisure Arts, Inc.

© 2014 by Leisure Arts, Inc.
104 Champs Boulevard, STE 100
Maumelle, AR 72113
www. leisurearts.com

ISBN: 978-1-4647-1595-2

Introduction

Have you looked at a lovely lace article and discovered, much to your chagrin, that the beautiful shawl—or even that lovely tablecloth—had been knitted! Much as you might want to duplicate a lovely piece of lace, making it by knitting would have to be too difficult. You may have thought of teaching yourself to knit lace—since you already knew how to knit—but learning to knit lace seemed to be an impossible feat.

You've come to the right place because lace knitting is a wonderful skill that actually consists of creating something out of blank space. All those beautiful patterns that you have admired in lace are created by deliberate holes which form patterns.

So follow along as we learn how to create those patterns, and after you have learned to make lace, why not turn your new skill on some of the knitted lace projects which we have for you starting on page 17.

Before You Begin

Some things you need to know to begin lace knitting.

THE TOOLS YOU NEED FOR LACE KNITTING

One of the great advantages of knitting lace is the realization that you won't need a lot of tools. If you were interested in building furniture, you'd need axes, saws, nails and a whole lot of other tools. To learn to knit lace, all you really need are some knitting needles and some yarn or thread.

NEEDLES

While you don't need special needles to knit lace, you may want to think about what kinds of needles will not only give you the best result but may just make your work faster and easier.

The first thing you should consider when choosing your needles for a lace project is how pointy is the tip of the needle. In lace knitting, you will be working two (and sometimes three) stitches together. Unless the needle is very pointy, this simple lace technique may be difficult.

Decide whether you prefer a needle made of metal, wood or plastic. Metal needles (including aluminum, steel, nickel plated) are slick, and the stitches will be able to move quickly along a metal needle. They tend to be cool to the touch, and they are great for knitters who want to knit fast, as there is very little friction, thereby allowing the stitches to move rapidly across the needle. They very rarely will bend or break so they will last a long time. However, one of the disadvantages of using metal needles is that with the speed at which your stitches move, there is always the chance that the last group of stitches you made could slide right off the needle. This probably is not a problem for knitters who have been working with lace knit projects for a long time.

However, if you are just beginning , you may be happier with plastic needles or wood needles. These needles tend to grab the stitches as you work. While you may find that this slows down your knitting, you won't have to worry about stitches slipping off the needle. Plastic needles seem to be warm to the touch and permit the yarn to slide across the needle with ease, but they could have one major disadvantage, depending upon the needles you choose. There is great variation in plastic needles, but many plastic needles have blunt points or points that can wear down as you knit with them.

Wooden needles, including bamboo, are warm to the touch, but they do tend to grab the yarn as you work. Experienced knitters are often turned off by wood's ability to grip the yarn which slows down the work. Smaller sizes break easily, and larger sizes are heavy and can add to the weight of the project.

You will also need to decide between straight needles and circular needles. Straight needles are the most popular and most widely recognized type of needle. These needles are used almost entirely for knitting flat two-dimensional projects where the work is done back and forth in rows.

Circular needles consist of a length of flexible nylon cable or wire of varying lengths with two pointed needle tips at either end. It is actually the same as having two straight needles joined together. The tips can be made of metal, plastic or wood, allowing the knitter to choose her favorite.

Circular needles were originally developed to work in seamless rounds, creating a seamless tube as in the body of a sweater. In making a circular project, the knitting is joined as it is worked around and around. Many knitters today, however, now prefer a circular needle for flat knitting as well, working back and forth. It is especially useful when knitting a large lace project where the straight needles can't accommodate the number of required stitches, and the stitches are all bunched together across the row. With a circular needle, the stitches are spaced evenly, and the lace design becomes apparent as the work progresses.

If you do decide to use a circular needle for lace knitting projects, check carefully to make certain that the joins between the needle and the cable are secure. Make certain that the tips are pointy.

YARN AND THREAD

Traditionally when you thought of lace knitting, you imagined a lovely, floating piece of lace emerging from your knitting needles. The work was done with fine thread no thicker than a cobweb spun by a clever spider. Many of these pieces still exist today, but the chance that they are used everyday is very slight.

However, today there are a number of threads that can give you much of the same look. Several years ago the Craft Yarn Council, an organization made up of yarn companies and yarn publishers, decided to make it easier for yarn manufacturers, publishers and designers to prepare consumer friendly products and for consumers to select the right materials for a project by developing a standard yarn weight system. (See the chart on page 48.) Many of the threads used here for lace projects are listed in the Lace Weight (0) category.

Those threads in the Lace Weight (0) category are listed by number (the finer the threads, the larger the number). The most popular include 30, 20, 10, 5 and 3.

There are even finer threads available in other parts of the world, and if you were interested in recreating an antique lace knitting pattern, you might find it possible to substitute a vintage thread available up to size 100. Most lace knitters today who use the Lace Weight threads use Size 10. If you'd like to experience this thread, try the patterns on pages 24 and 37.

For those knitters who still want the look of that vintage lace but need added sturdiness, there are a multitude of yarns available in sizes 1 (Super Fine) and 2 (Fine). Patterns that use these yarns can be found on pages 21, 27, 34, 41 and 43.

If you are a knitter who loves the look of lace but wants something that could be knit and worn through the year, you can make your lace with even heavier weights. While the results won't be the same as a project knit with spider-web yarn, they will still retain the look and feel of a lace project. Check the scarf on page 30. And finally, if you love the look of lace, why not take a lace pattern and just knit yourself a lace afghan with a worsted weight yarn (page 44).

The Making of Lace

Lace knitting is a wonderful skill that actually consists of creating something out of a blank space. All those beautiful patterns in lace are created by deliberate holes which form a decorative pattern. Those holes or eyelets are formed by working an increase and then a decrease somewhere probably in the same row.

The stitches formed by the decreases either slant to the right or slant to the left. The slanting stitches become part of the design, and if the decrease happens to be several stitches away from the increase, that whole area will slant in the desired direction.

INCREASES
Yarn Over

While there are many stitches used in lace knitting, there is one stitch that is used most of the time to make an increase: the yarn over (or as it is called in a pattern, a YO).

The yarn over is basically just a loop of yarn or thread that goes over the top of the working needle, moving first in front of the needle and then down in the back.

The yarn over always begins with the thread in front of the needle. So, therefore if you are making a YO after a knit stitch, you must first bring the thread forward as if to purl, then wrap the thread over the needle and knit the next stitch.

A yarn over can be made after a purl stitch as well. The thread will be in the correct spot in the front of the needle. Take the thread over the top of the right needle,

and then bring it between the two needles to the front again. The needle is once again in position to purl the next stitch.

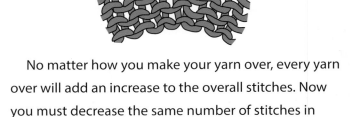

No matter how you make your yarn over, every yarn over will add an increase to the overall stitches. Now you must decrease the same number of stitches in order to make the work even.

DECREASES

There are basically two types of decreases: left-slanting and right-slanting. They do exactly what you'd expect them to do: they either slant the work to the left or to the right.

Right-Slanting Decreases
Knit 2 together (k2tog)

Work to the place where the decrease is to be made, then insert the tip of the right-hand needle from left to right through the fronts of the two stitches on the left-hand needle. Wrap the thread around as if you were knitting one stitch. One stitch has now been decreased.

Purl 2 together (P2tog)

In much the same way, you can purl 2 stitches together. Insert the right-hand needle from *right* to *left* through the fronts of two purl stitches on the left-hand needle. Wrap the working thread around as if you were purling one stitch. One stitch has now been decreased.

Left-Slanting Decreases

Slip, slip, knit (ssk)

Once again, work to the place where you wish to make the decrease. Slip the next two stitches, one at a time, as if to knit to the right needle.

Insert the left needle into the fronts of these two stitches and knit them together. One stitch is decreased.

Slip, slip, purl (ssp)

In much the same way as Slip, slip, knit (ssk), slip the two stitches one at a time as if to knit to the right needle. Purl them together through the back loops. One stitch is decreased.

Knit 2 together through back loops (K2tog tbl)

With the right needle behind the left needle, insert the right needle through the back loops of the next two stitches on the needle. Knit the two stitches together.

The K2tog tbl is probably the easiest way to achieve a left-slanting decrease.

Slip 1, Knit 1, Pass the slipped Stitch Over (sl 1, K1, PSSO or SKPO)

Insert the right-hand needle, as if to knit, into the stitch, slip this stitch onto the right-hand needle without knitting it, then knit the next stitch.

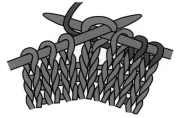

Using the left-hand needle, lift the slipped stitch over the knitted stitch and off the needle. One stitch is decreased.

Decreases Without Slants

In some projects the instructions will call for two increases (2 yarn overs) one on either side of a decrease. This will decrease 3 stitches into 1 stitch.

Slip 1, Knit 2 Together, Pass the slipped Stitch Over (sl 1, K2tog, PSSO)

Insert the right-hand needle, as if to knit, into the stitch, slip this stitch onto the right-hand needle without knitting it, then knit the next 2 stitches together.

Using the left-hand needle, lift the slipped stitch over the knitted stitch and off the needle. One Stitch is decreased.

Beginning and Completing a Project

GAUGE

Knitters have always been encouraged to produce a gauge swatch usually of about 4" before beginning a project. This procedure was to make certain that the gauge given in the pattern was accurate. Otherwise it is possible you might not have enough yarn and your knitted garment might not fit. This may seem a bit ridiculous if you are knitting a bit of lace that is not intended to fit anyone, such as a lace scarf, like the one on page 19. But, making a gauge swatch is really a great idea for a number of reasons. First of all, a swatch will give you a good idea of how the finished project will look so you can make certain that your thread might be a good choice.

If you have never made a gauge swatch before, start now. If you have always made a gauge swatch when knitting an ordinary knit project, creating a gauge swatch for a lace project where you have to account for all of those yarn overs and stitches knitted together might be a little different.

The swatch should be worked over two complete pattern repeats along with several stitches on each side of the swatch and a few rows at the top and bottom to make a square that will hold its shape. For instance, if you are making a gauge swatch for the Scarf of Many Colors on page 27, begin by casting on 35 stitches in the thread called for in the pattern. This pattern calls for a multiple of 10 stitches plus 1, which equals 21 stitches for 2 repeats. Add 2 stitches for the left side of the swatch and 2 for the right. Begin by knitting 2 rows, then begin the pattern, adding 2 knit stitches at the beginning of each row and 2 at the end of each row. When you have completed about 4 inches, add 2 rows of knitting at the bottom and bind off the swatch. Place the swatch on a flat surface and pin it out. Be careful not to stretch the knitting. Measure the outside edges; ideally the sample should be a square of at least 4".

Now measure the center 2" and count the actual stitches and rows per inch. If you have more stitches or rows per inch than listed in the pattern, make another gauge swatch with larger size needles. If you have fewer stitches or rows per inch than specified make another swatch with smaller size needles. Once you have begun a pattern, it's not a bad idea to check your gauge every few inches. Sometimes if you become very relaxed, your knitting can become looser; if you become tense, your knitting can become tighter. To keep your gauge, you might need to change needles in the middle of a project.

BLOCKING

When you have completed working a piece of knitted lace, you will need to block your project. The method that you use to block will depend a large part on what was used to work the piece. No matter the method, however, the end result will be that you will have opened the design and allowed all of those beautiful lacy pieces to shine.

There are three basic methods for blocking: **wet blocking**, **spray blocking** or **steam blocking**. The method you choose to use for your project is actually determined by the type of thread or yarn you used to knit a particular project. Here are some suggestions:

Cotton: wet block or steam

Linen: wet block or steam

Mohair: wet block or steam

Synthetics (acrylics): spraying; do not press

Wool: wet block or spraying

Wool blends: wet block or spraying; do not press

Always carefully follow the manufacturer's care instructions on the yarn label. No matter what method you choose to use, the technique is basically the same. The piece is dampened, placed on a flat surface, either pinned or just placed into the proper position and allowed to dry.

Blocking Supplies

1. A blocking board: a large flat surface, large enough to hold knitted piece. Cover the surface with plastic or towels.
2. Rust-proof pins
3. Spray bottle with cold water (for spray blocking), basin with water (for wet blocking), steam iron or handheld steamer (for steam blocking)
4. Tape measure to determine correct size
5. Colorfast towels
6. Pressing cloth

Wet Blocking

If your knitting has become soiled or discolored as you worked it, you may wish to carefully wash the piece in cool water, following the manufacturer's instructions. If washing is not necessary, just soak the project in some cool water. Carefully squeeze the water out of the knitting and lay the project on a clean towel. Roll the towel, pressing out as much water as possible. If necessary, you may want to repeat the process with another clean towel. Lay the project on the blocking board and pull it into the desired shape. Pin it to the blocking board and allow the knitting to air dry.

Spray Blocking

In this method you eliminate washing or soaking. Instead you lay the piece down on the blocking board, stretch it out to the required shape and pin it in shape. Then you spray the knitting with a spray bottle filled with water. If you prefer, you can spray the piece first, then stretch it out to the required shape and pin it in place. This is the most gentle blocking technique and probably the easiest to do.

Steam Blocking

There are two ways to block your knitting by steaming. In the first you pin your knitted project to the desired measurements, making sure that the wrong side is facing up. Place a damp, thin towel on top. Then with your household iron at its highest setting, press down very lightly, which will force the steam out. The other way to steam block is to take your iron or—if you have

one—a handheld steamer, set to the proper setting for steam and hold it over the knitting allowing the steam to penetrate the project until the knitting is damp. With this method you do not allow the iron to touch the stitches. While you are steaming, pull your project to the desired shape. Allow the knitting to dry. It's probably not a good idea to use steam blocking on any synthetic fibers because the steam could possibly melt the fibers.

STARCHING

Some lace projects, especially those made with thin crochet threads, have a more finished look when they have been starched. Here is what you will need in addition to the supplies listed above if you would like to starch your project.

1. Stiffening Solution. Use one of the ones listed below:
   A. Equal amounts of water and commercial stiffening solution (available at a craft store), thoroughly mixed.
   B. Equal amounts of white craft glue and water, thoroughly mixed.
   C. Thick solution of commercial boilable starch (liquid or spray starches won't work)
2. Plastic bag. Use a plastic bag that locks across the top for mixing the solution.

STARCHING INSTRUCTIONS

Step 1: Wash the finished project by hand with a mild soap. Rinse carefully in warm water.

Step 2: Pour the prepared stiffening solution into a plastic bag and place in a bowl. If your project can't fit in your plastic bag, pour the solution into the bowl. Immerse your project in the solution and allow it to soak for about a minute. Remove and press out any extra solution. Do not squeeze, the project should be very wet, but there should be no solution in the decorative holes. You can store any excess stiffener.

Step 3: Place the project on the blocking board and pin into shape.

No matter which blocking method you choose, the key to success is to allow your knitting to dry thoroughly while it is still pinned in place.

Aids for the Lace Knitter

No one has ever said that lace knitting is easy, but everyone who has ever tried it certainly agrees that it can be enjoyable, especially if you have a few quiet helpers. While there are probably a number of tools that might help make a lace knitter's life easier, the two helpers that are a "must" are the "stitch marker" and the "Lifeline".

STITCH MARKERS

A purchased stitch marker is a little round item, usually made of plastic or metal that can be slipped onto the knitting needle to mark a certain place in the row. There are many different sizes and shapes of stitch markers, some quite decorative and elegant. My personal favorite stitch marker is a piece of yarn in a contrasting color. I cut a piece about 4" or 5", tie it on the needle and move it whenever I pass it. I never knit into the marker!

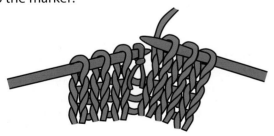

What does the stitch marker do? Basically the stitch marker tells you exactly where you are in a pattern, and that's something anyone working in lace knitting will tell you it is important to know. Placing a stitch marker between each repeat of a lace pattern will help you maintain the correct number of stitches in each repeat across a row or round. It also helps you find where you might have made an error in the previous row. For instance, if you are working a lace pattern with 13 repeats, and each repeat is 12 stitches, you are going to have to keep track of 156 stitches. That's a lot of constant counting to make sure that you haven't added or lost stitches. Now, place a stitch marker (either one of those purchased markers or a piece of yarn) between each repeat. Instead of constantly counting 156 stitches, you have only 13 groups of 12 stitches each.

As you check each group between the markers, you might find an error in one group. Maybe you forgot to make a YO.

How much easier will it be to make the correction in one of your groups than to knit the entire row and then try to figure out where the mistake happened. So, save yourself a lot of time and frustration. Use those markers. Check to make certain that the proper number of stitches are between the markers.

LIFELINES

Knitting lace is fun! Just so long as you don't have to deal with knitting nightmares!

You pick up your knitting and you discover that a needle has slipped out, and the stitches are starting to unravel. How many rows have you lost? Where do you begin?

Or, you discover that you have more (or fewer) stitches on your needle. There's obviously a mistake several rows back.

Now you realize that you're going to have to rip the knitting back several rows (or even just one row). Those beautiful decreases and yarn overs that make a piece of knitted lace so beautiful have now turned your hard work into a miserable mess. As you begin to rip back, the stitches you worked so hard to produce are disappearing, and all the work you have put into your knitting is unraveling as you move. "Help! Someone, please throw me a lifeline!" If you were smart, you would have made your own lifeline. It is simply a length of contrasting thread placed through the stitches of a row or round that you know has been done correctly. Then if you need to rip back to find your error, just rip back to that row.

Here's how you do it: cut a piece of a smooth cotton contrasting yarn or thread that is about 4" or 5" (10 cm or 12.7 cm) longer than your row or round and thread it onto a tapestry needle. Choose a row that you know has no mistakes. If your pattern calls for making a row without any YOs, that would be the best choice. Now, leaving the knitting on the needle, slip the tapestry needle along the row through each stitch on the knitting needle as if you were transferring those stitches. **But, don't slip your stitches off the knitting needle.** You have made yourself a Lifeline. One of the good choices for a Lifeline is dental floss. It is strong and slips easily through the stitches. You're probably not going to confuse dental floss with yarn either.

Be certain that your Lifeline is long enough so that there are a few inches hanging over the sides. Some knitters even like to tie the two ends of the Lifeline together so that the Lifeline doesn't get pulled out before it is used. Make a note of which row the Lifeline has been threaded through; that will make it easier to find your row in a complicated pattern.

Once you have installed the Lifeline, continue knitting as normal. Be very careful that you do not accidentally knit the Lifeline together with the yarn you are using for your project. You can add a new Lifeline every few inches, leaving the old Lifeline in place or removing it when you no longer feel it is necessary.

Now, if you suddenly discover that you are missing a stitch, or you obviously have made some other mistake, you can use your Lifeline. Simply remove your stitches from the knitting needle and rip out the rows since your Lifeline was inserted. The Lifeline will catch the stitches and prevent you from ripping further. Now slip the stitches back onto the knitting needle in order and continue re-working the pattern. Make certain that you start at the proper end, and be very careful that you don't knit the Lifeline along with the row. You may want to keep the Lifeline in place for a few rows just to make certain that you're not going to repeat that error.

Knitting from Charts

Charts for both knitting and crocheting have been used for about 100 years in most countries of the world except for the English speaking world where the choice has always been the printed word.

Japan has always been the country best known for the use of symbols both for crochet and knitting. Until 1955, publishing companies and knit and crochet teachers in Japan used their own symbols. That year the Japanese Industrial Standards Committee (JISC) was called upon to establish some standards. Members of that group at the time included the Japan Knitting License Society, one of the largest knitting associations of Japan, and the NAC Japan Knitting Association.

The first standards were established by that group on May 21, 1955 with a final revision made on November 1, 1995. Today the JISC continues to be responsible for symbols and their use. In Japan, knitting charts are completely standardized by JISC, and knitting instructions are well regulated.

Unfortunately, the universal symbols for knitting have not been readily adapted in most of the world as crochet symbols have. Different countries today often use their own symbols. In the United States, different books and magazines use different symbols. Luckily for all of us, when symbols are published in a pattern in the United States, a key is usually given with the chart as on page14.

I once heard a knitting chart described as a road map, which is a perfect description. It's not going to tell you what beautiful sites you might see on either side of the road, but if you follow the path laid out for you, the end will be worth the trip. We've given you some "road maps" for knit stitches to practice reading knitting symbols on pages 14 and 15. Try following the chart; then check your results with the printed version on page 16.

The list of knitting symbols can be long and involved. Fortunately most knitted lace usually requires fewer symbols. Here is a list of those symbols used most often in knitted lace patterns.

☐	Knit on right side, Purl on wrong side
⊡	Purl on right side, Knit on wrong side
◿	K2tog on right side, P2tog on wrong side
◺	P2tog on right side, K2tog on wrong side
⊙	yarn over
◺	slip, slip, Knit (SSK)
◿	slip 1, K2tog, PSSO (SK2P)
⊠	slip1, Knit 1, PSSO (SKPO)
◿	Knit 2 together through back loop (K2tog tbl)
◣	Purl 2 together through back loop (P2tog tbl)
☑	slip
☐	repeat

Let's follow our road map/chart (Number 6) on page 15. The printed instructions spell out the multiple: the basic repeat or the stitches needed to work one complete unit of the pattern. It also gives you the additional stitches added at the beginning or end of a row. On the chart, the multiple (the basic repeat), appears between the red lines and the additional stitches are on either side of the red lines. Before you begin to work, check the Key to determine which stitches will be used and how they will be shown.

The chart begins at the lower right-hand corner (which is the exact opposite of reading this text). The bottom row, a right side row, is the first row of knitting, and you work your way to the top left. So the second (and all even rows) are read from left to right, while the first and all odd rows are read from right to left. If you are reading a chart for knitting in the round, however, each row is a right side row, worked from right to left.

Our sample chart here is for a lace pattern that has 12 (9 + 3) stitches across and is 4 rows long. The key tells you that you will use five different stitches to make this pattern: knit, purl, ssk (slip, slip, knit), K2tog (knit 2 together) and YO (Yarn over).

Row 1 is a right side row so it will be read from right to left. This row will contain the first increases (yarn overs) and the first decreases (SSK and K2tog). The stitch count of 9 stitches will remain the same because every decrease (either an SSK or a K2tog) has an increase (a yarn over). The stitch count, therefore shown by the 9 boxes between the red lines remains the same.

The row begins with two blank squares, which the key tells you are two knit stitches. Now the repeat begins with a yarn over, then there are two more blanks to indicate two knit stitches followed by an SSK and a K2tog. Finally the row ends with two more knit stitches, a yarn over, a knit stitch and the final knit stitch outside of the multiple.

Row 2 is a wrong side row so it will be read from left to right. The row begins with a square with a dot in it. This will tell you that this is a knit stitch on a wrong side row. The rest of the row to the last stitch are blank squares. Because this is on the wrong side, those blank squares are now purl stitches. The row ends with another knit stitch.

Row 3 (a right side row) does something that lace knitting often does. This row will "borrow" a stitch at the beginning of the row and then return it at the end of the row. In this way, the lace pattern is moved across the row. So instead of beginning with two knit stitches at the beginning of the row (outside the red line), it has one knit stitch outside the box, and then the first yarn over, followed by two knit stitches, and an SSK, which means that you have subtracted the stitch added with the yarn over.

Now add a K2tog and two knit stitches. At this point, we are missing a stitch. Never fear! The next stitch is a yarn over, which evens out the missing stitch. The multiple (within the red line) ends with a knit stitch. The row, however, ends with two knit stitches outside of the red line. Everything has come out even; you started the row with nine stitches plus 3, and you end it with 9 plus 3.

The important thing in working from a chart is to work every stitch as it appears in the box. Do not be concerned that the SSK asks you to work two stitches, but there is only one box. Just work the SSK because someplace on the row, there will be a yarn over to make it all come out even. Our "road map" doesn't show you what the scenery looks like; it tells you what you will find when you arrive. Each row shows you what the row will look like after it has been completed.

As you work more stitches with lace knitting charts, you will discover one more little "problem." Occasionally a pattern will have a row where the increases and decreases are *not* matched in the same row. In that case, a box where nothing is happening is shaded indicating that there is no stitch here. Just keep working the stitch before the shaded box and after the shaded box. No matter how complicated a lace chart may seem, keep following the road to the end. The decreases and increases don't have to be next to each other—or even in the same row—but they will all work together if you just have faith!

The little chart and the key take up much less room and much less time to read than the written pattern on page 16. On pages 14 and 15 are a number of charts with the instructions printed out. Try practicing reading and working these charts. Check the written instructions on page 16 and the photo to see how easy working from charts can be. Once you can read charts and work from them, you have opened yourself to patterns from places all over the world. You may not be able to say as much as "hello" in other languages, but you'll be able to create beautiful knitted lace from designers around the world.

How To Read a Knit Chart Pattern

Try to create the sample stitching using the chart and key. Then check your work using the written instructions on page 16.

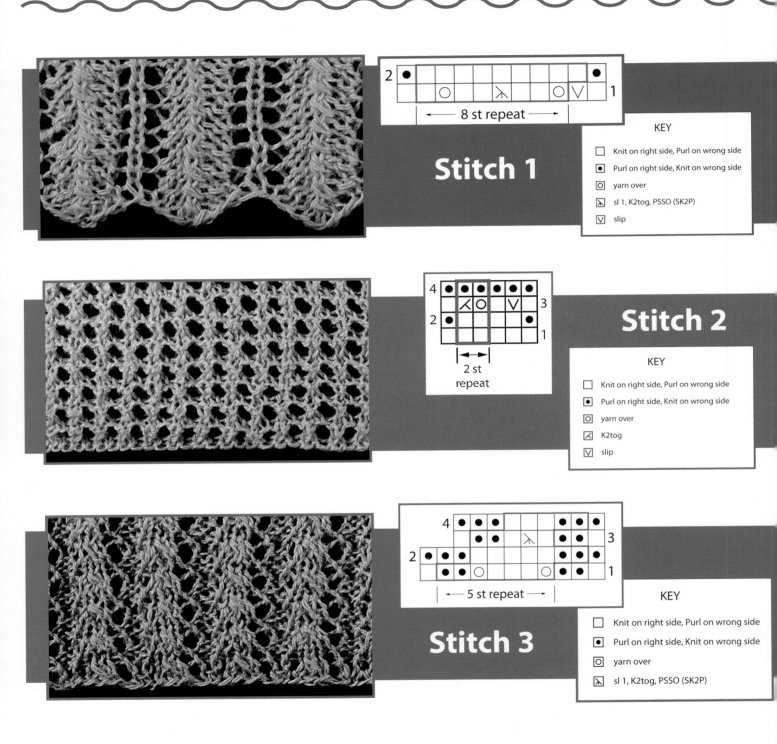

Stitch 1

8 st repeat

KEY

- ☐ Knit on right side, Purl on wrong side
- ⊡ Purl on right side, Knit on wrong side
- ⊙ yarn over
- ⋏ sl 1, K2tog, PSSO (SK2P)
- ⋁ slip

Stitch 2

2 st repeat

KEY

- ☐ Knit on right side, Purl on wrong side
- ⊡ Purl on right side, Knit on wrong side
- ⊙ yarn over
- ⋉ K2tog
- ⋁ slip

Stitch 3

5 st repeat

KEY

- ☐ Knit on right side, Purl on wrong side
- ⊡ Purl on right side, Knit on wrong side
- ⊙ yarn over
- ⋏ sl 1, K2tog, PSSO (SK2P)

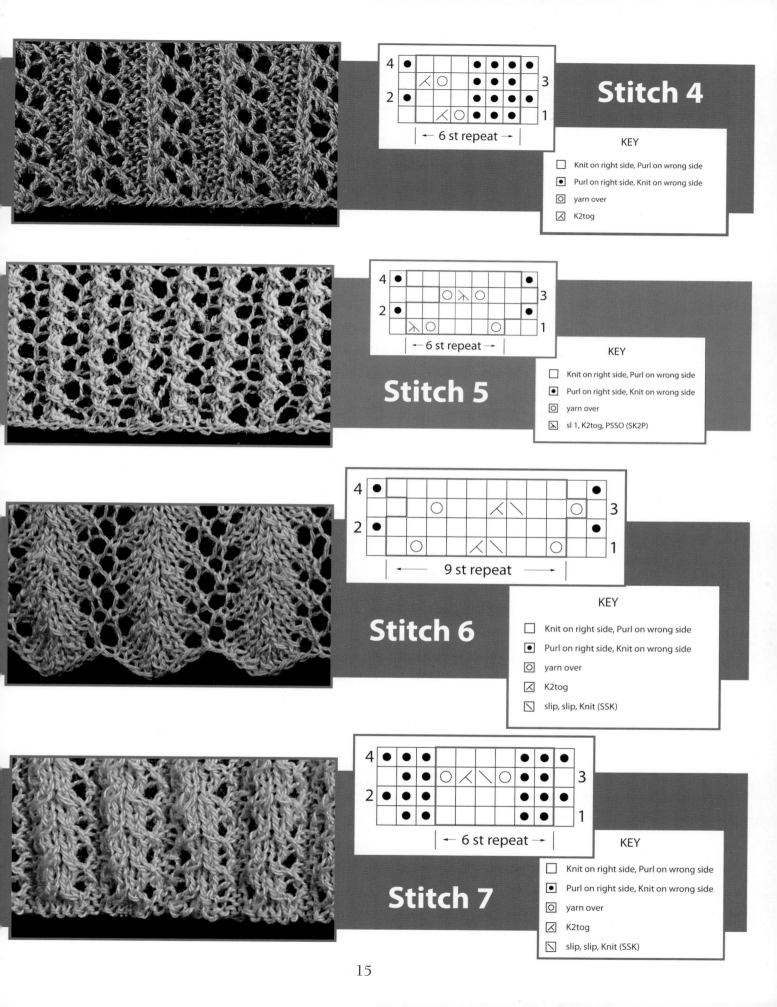

Stitch 4

4	●				●	●	●	●	
		�METER	○		●	●	●		3
2	●				●	●	●	●	
			⟋	○	●	●	●		1

|← 6 st repeat →|

KEY

☐ Knit on right side, Purl on wrong side

● Purl on right side, Knit on wrong side

○ yarn over

⟋ K2tog

Stitch 5

4	●								●	
				○	⟋	○			●	3
2	●								●	
		⟋		○				○		1

|← 6 st repeat →|

KEY

☐ Knit on right side, Purl on wrong side

● Purl on right side, Knit on wrong side

○ yarn over

⟑ sl 1, K2tog, PSSO (SK2P)

Stitch 6

4	●										●	
				○			⟋	⟍		○		●	3
2	●										●	
			○				⟋	⟍			○		1

|← 9 st repeat →|

KEY

☐ Knit on right side, Purl on wrong side

● Purl on right side, Knit on wrong side

○ yarn over

⟋ K2tog

⟍ slip, slip, Knit (SSK)

Stitch 7

4	●	●	●						●	●	●	
		●	●	○	⟋	⟍	○		●	●		3
2	●	●	●						●	●	●	
		●	●						●	●		1

|← 6 st repeat →|

KEY

☐ Knit on right side, Purl on wrong side

● Purl on right side, Knit on wrong side

○ yarn over

⟋ K2tog

⟍ slip, slip, Knit (SSK)

Stitch 1
Multiple 8+3

Row 1: (right side): K1, sl 1; *YO, K2, sl 1, K2tog, PSSO, K2, YO, K1; rep from * to last st, K1.

Row 2: K1, purl to last st, K1.

Repeat Rows 1 and 2 for pattern.

Stitch 2
Multiple: 2+ 4

Row 1 (right side): Knit.

Row 2: K1, purl to last st, K1.

Row 3: K1, sl 1, K1; *YO, K2tog; rep from * to last st, K1.

Row 4: Knit.

Repeat Rows 1 through 4 for pattern.

Stitch 3
Multiple 5 + 4

Row 1 (right side): K1, P2; *YO, K3, YO, P2; rep from * to last st, K1.

Row 2: K3; *P5, K2; rep from * to last st, K1.

Row 3: K1, P2; *K1, sl 1, K2tog, PSSO, K1, P2; rep from * to last st, K1.

Row 4: K3; *P3, K2; rep from * to last st, K1.

Repeat Rows 1 through 4 for pattern.

Stitch 4
Multiple: 6+ 2

Row 1 (right side): K1; *P3, YO, K2tog, K1; rep from * to last st, K1.

Row 2: K1; *P3, K3; rep from * to last st, K1.

Row 3: K1; *P3, K1, YO, K2tog; rep from * to lasts st, K1.

Row 4: K1; *P3, K3; rep from * to last st, K1.

Repeat Rows 1 through 4 for pattern.

Stitch 5
Multiple: 6+3

Row 1 (right side): K2 *YO, K3, YO, sl 1, K2tog, PSSO; rep from * to last st, K1.

Row 2: K1, purl to last st, K1.

Row 3: *K3, YO, sl 1, K2tog, PSSO, YO; rep from * across to last 3 sts, K3.

Row 4: Rep Row 2.

Repeat Rows 1 through 4 for pattern.

Stitch 6
Multiple: 9+ 3

Row 1 (right side): K2; *YO, K2, SSK, K2tog, K2, YO, K1; rep from * to last st, K1.

Row 2: K1, purl to last stitch, K1.

Row 3: K1; *YO, K2, SSK, K2tog, K2, YO, K1; rep from * to last 2 sts, K2.

Row 4: Rep Row 2.

Repeat Rows 1 through 4 for pattern.

Stitch 7
Multiple: 6 + 4

Row 1: K1; *P2, K4; rep from * to last 3 sts, P2, K1.

Row 2: K3; *P4, K2; rep from * to last st, K1.

Row 3: K1: *P2, YO, SSK, K2tog, YO; rep from * to last 3 sts, P2, K1.

Row 4: Rep Row 2.

Repeat Rows 1 through 4 for pattern.

Lace Knit Projects

Now you can practice all of the lace knitting skills we've shown you in the first part of our book. Here are 14 projects, ranging from an easy edging to an heirloom doily.

If you're not ready to tackle knitting with fine threads, why not try making one of the projects, such as the Lacy Hat or the Winter Lace Afghan, that use all of the techniques of lace knitting with heavier weight yarns.

If you'd like to practice knitting from charts, you'll find several projects here that include knitting charts.

Lace Scarf

*A great project for practicing a lace knit pattern, this scarf can be
worn as a shawl into the spring warmer weather.*

SKILL LEVEL

Easy ⬛⬛◻◻

SIZE

Approx. 15" x 59" (38 cm x 150 cm)

MATERIALS

Super Fine Yarn

[70% wool superwash, 30% nylon, 1.76 ounces, 213
yards (50 grams, 195 meters)] per ball
4 balls white

Note: *Photographed model made with Red Heart® Heart
& Sole®, #3115 Ivory*

Size 5 (3.75 mm) knitting needles (or size required for
gauge)
Stitch markers
Yarn needle

GAUGE

22 sts = 4" (10 cm)

INSTRUCTIONS

Note: *There is a seed stitch (K1, P1) border worked on all of
the edges, and a lace pattern worked between the borders.
The border is worked on the first and last 4 rows as well as
the first 4 and last 4 sts of each row.*

CO 80 sts

Row 1 (wrong side): *K1, P1; rep from * across

Row 2: *P1, K1; rep from * across,

Rows 3 and 4: Rep Rows 1 and 2.

Row 5 (wrong side): [K1, P1] twice (for Seed Stitch
border) place marker, purl to last 4 sts, place marker [K1,
P1] twice (for Seed Stitch border).

Row 6: [P1, K1] twice, slip marker, *YO, K2, K2tog, K2;
rep from * to next marker, slip marker, [P1, K1] twice.

Row 7: [K1, P1] twice, slip marker, purl to next marker,
slip marker, [K1, P1] twice.

Row 8: [Pl, K1] twice, slip marker, *K2, K2tog, K2, YO; rep
from * to next marker, slip marker, [P1, K1] twice.

Row 9: [K1, P1] twice, slip marker, purl to next marker,
slip marker, [K1, P1] twice.

Rep Rows 6-9 until the piece measures about 58 ½"
(148.5 cm) from beginning, end with a wrong side row.
Then work the following seed stitch border:

Seed Stitch Border

Row 1 (right side): *P1 ,K1; rep from * across.

Row 2: *K1, P1; rep from * across.

Rows 3 and 4: Rep Rows 1 and 2.

BO. Weave in ends.

Crescent Shawl

Designed by Julie Farmer for Red Heart®

A lovely little lace knit shawlette will add style and warmth all year long.

SKILL LEVEL

Easy ▢▢▢▢▢

SIZE

Approx. 64" (163 cm) x 10" (26 cm)

MATERIALS

Super Fine Yarn

[70% wool superwash, 30% nylon, 1.76 ounces, 213 yards (50 grams, 195 meters)] per ball

      2 balls white

Note: *Photographed model made with Red Heart®*
Heart & Sole®, #3115 Ivory

Size 6 (4 mm) knitting needles (or size required for gauge)

GAUGE

22 sts = 4 ¾" (12 cm) in lace pattern

STITCH GUIDE

SSK (slip, slip, knit): Slip next two stitches as if to knit, one at a time, to right-hand needle. Insert tip of left-hand needle into fronts of these sts from left to right. Knit them together through back loop: 1 stitch decreased.

P2tog tbl: Purl 2 sts together through back loop.

LACE PATTERN

Note: *Stitch count will increase 1 st on right side rows and decrease 1 st on wrong side rows for each repeat.*

Row 1 (right side): *K4, YO, K1 , YO, K4, K2tog; rep from *.

Rows 2, 4, 6, 8 and 10: *P2tog, P10; rep from * across.

Row 3: *K5, YO, K1, YO, K3, K2tog; rep from * across.

Row 5: *K6, YO, K1, YO, K2, K2tog; rep from * across.

Row 7: *K7, YO, K1, YO, K1, K2tog; rep from * across.

Row 9: *K8, YO, K1, YO, K2tog; rep from * across.

Row 11: *SSK, K4, YO, K1, YO, K4; rep from * across.

Rows 12,14,16 and 18: *P10, P2togtbl; rep from * across.

Row 13: *SSK, K3, YO, K1, YO, K5; rep from * across.

Row 15: *SSK, K2, YO, K1, YO, K6; rep from * across.

Row 17: *SSK, K1, YO, K1, YO, K7; rep from * across.

Row 19: *SSK, YO, K1 ,YO, K8; rep from * across.

Row 20: *P10, P2tog tbl; rep from * across.

INSTRUCTIONS

Note: *Short Row Shaping begins at Row 35.*

CO 286 sts.

Rows 1 through 20: Work Rows 1 through 20 of Lace Pattern.

Rows 21 through 30: Work Rows 1 through 10 of Lace Pattern.

Row 31 (right side): Knit across.

Instructions continue on page 22.

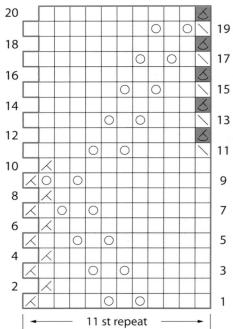

KEY

☐ Knit on right side, Purl on wrong side

☒ K2tog on right side, P2tog on wrong side

◯ yarn over

◻ slip, slip, Knit (SSK)

◼ Purl 2 together through back loop (P2tog tbl)

← 11 st repeat →

Row 32: P143, place marker, purl to end.

Row 33: Knit.

Row 34: Purl

Row 35: Knit to marker, SSK, K5, turn.

Row 36: Purl to marker, P2tog, P5, turn.

Row 37: Knit to 1 st before last turn, SSK, K5, turn.

Row 38: Purl to 1 st before last turn, P2tog, P5, turn.

Rep Rows 37 and 38 until there are 9 sts left after a P2tog on a wrong-side, purl to end of row.

Next Row: Knit across to 1 st before last turn, SSK, knit to end of row: 239 sts

Knit 3 rows.

Bind off. Weave in ends.

Coaster

Want to practice knitting lace in a circle?
Try making this little coaster.

SKILL LEVEL

Easy ◼◼☐☐

SIZE

Approx. 3" (7.62 cm) across

MATERIALS

Size 10 crochet thread

[100% cotton, 400 yards (365 meters)] per ball
      1 ball white (or ecru)

Note: *Photographed model made with*
    Aunt Lydia's® Classic Crochet Thread,
      size 10 #419 Ecru

Stitch Markers
Four Size 1 (2.25 cm) double point knitting needles
    (or size required for gauge)
16" Size 1 (2.25 cm) Circular knitting needle

Note: *Begin coaster with double-point needles and switch to circular needle when the number of stitches increases.*

Gauge

18 sts = 2" (5.08 cm) in circular St st (knit each row)

INSTRUCTIONS

Note: Mark the start of each rnd with a marker.

Cast on 9 sts onto one double-point needle. Divide the sts onto three needles; join, being careful not to twist sts.

Rnds 1 and 2: Knit.

Rnd 3: *YO, K1; rep from * around: 18sts.

Rnds 4 through 6: Knit.

Rnd 7: Rep Rnd 3: 36 sts.

Rnds 8 through 10: Knit.

Rnd 11: K1; *YO, K1, YO, K3; rep from * around, ending last rep with K2: 54 sts.

Rnds 12 through 14: Knit.

Rnd 15: P1: *(YO, K1) 3 times, YO, P3; rep from * around, ending last rep with P2: 90 sts.

Rnds 16 through 18: Knit.

Bind off.

Heirloom Flower Doily

*A great way to show your knitting skill: make a knitted piece that is sure
to become a family heirloom.*

SKILL LEVEL

Experienced ■ ■ ■ ■

SIZE

Approx. 8" (20.32 cm) across

MATERIALS

Size 10 crochet thread

[100% Viscose from Bamboo, 300 yards (276 meters)]
   per ball

      1 ball ecru

Note: *Photographed model made with Aunt Lydia's®
   Bamboo Crochet Thread, size 10 #226 Natural*

Stitch Markers

Five Size 1 (2.25 mm) double point knitting needles (or
   size required for gauge)

16" Size 1 (2.25 mm) circular knitting needle (or size
   required for gauge)

Note: *Begin doily with double-point needles and switch to
circular needle when the number of stitches increases.*

GAUGE

16 sts = 2" (5.08 cm) (in circular St st (knit each row)

INSTRUCTIONS

Note: *Mark the start of each round with a marker.*

Cast on 8 sts onto one double-point needle. Divide the stitches evenly onto the four double point needles; join, being careful not to twist sts. Knit one round.

Rnds 1 and 2: Knit around.

Rnd 3: *YO, K1; rep from * around: 16 sts.

Rnds 4 through 6: Knit.

Rnd 7: *YO, K1; rep from * around: 32 sts.

Rnds 8 through 12: Knit.

Rnd 13: *K2tog, (YO) twice, SK2P; rep from * around.

Rnd 14 * K1, drop next YO, (K1 [P1, K1] 4 times) all in next YO, K1; rep from * around : 88 sts.

Rnds 15 through 24: Knit.

Rnd 25: * YO, K11; rep from * around : 96 sts.

Rnd 26: Knit.

Rnd 27: * Y0, K1, YO, K11; rep from * around : 112 sts.

Rnd 28: Knit.

Rnd 29: * Y0, K3, YO, K4, SK2P, K4; rep from * around : 112 sts.

Rnd 30: Knit.

Rnd 31: * YO, K1, YO, SK2P, YO, K1, YO, K3, SK2P, K3; rep from * around : 112 sts.

Rnd 32: Knit.

Rnd 33: * YO, K3, YO, (K1, P1) all in next st, YO, K3, YO, K2, SK2P, K2; rep from * around : 136 sts.

Rnd 34: Knit.

Rnd 35: * YO, K1, YO, SK2P, YO, K4, YO, SK2P, (YO, K1) twice, SK2P, K1; rep from * around: 136 sts.

Rnd 36: Knit.

Rnd 37: * YO, K3, YO, K2, slip 1, K1, PSSO, K2tog, K2, YO, K3, YO, SK2P; rep from * around: 136 sts.

Rnd 38: Knit.

Rnd 39: * YO, K1, YO, SK2P, YO, K2, sl 1, K1, PSSO, K2tog, K2, YO, SK2P , (yo, K1) twice; rep from * around : 136 sts.

Rnd 40: Knit.

Rnd 41: K1, * K2tog, YO, K2tog, **Turn**, P1, (K1 [P1, K1] twice) all in next st, P1, slip 1, **Turn**, bind off 7 sts (scallop made) :1 st remains on right hand needle; rep from * to last 3 sts; K2tog, YO, K1, **Turn**, P1, (K1, [P1, K1] twice) all in next st, P1, sl 1, **Turn**, bind off 7 sts. Fasten off remaining st.

Scarf of Many Colors

Designed by Scarlet Taylor for Red Heart®

Not only is this lovely lace scarf easy to knit, but it is made with self-striping yarn that will change the colors as if by magic.

SKILL LEVEL

Easy ▣▣▢▢

SIZE

Approx. 4 ½" x 60" (11.43 cm x 152.40 cm)

MATERIALS

Super Fine Yarn Super Fine 1

[70% wool superwash, 30% nylon, 1.76 ounces, 213 yards (50 grams, 195 meters)] per ball

    2 balls multi color

Note: *Photographed model made with Red Heart® Heart & Sole®, #3970 Faded Jeans*

Size 2 (2.75 mm) knitting needles (or size required for gauge)

Yarn needle

GAUGE

32 sts = 4" (10 cm) in Lace Pattern

STITCH GUIDE

SK2P: Slip 1, K2tog, pass the slipped stitch over the knit stitch.

INSTRUCTIONS

There is a garter stitch border (knit each stitch) worked on all of the edges and a lace pattern worked between the borders. The border is worked on the first and last two rows as well as the first 2 and last 2 sts of each row.

Lace Pattern (multiple of 10 sts plus 1)

Rows 1 and 3 (wrong side): Purl across.

Row 2: K1, *YO, K3, SK2P, K3, YO, K1; rep from * across .

Row 4: P1, *K1, YO, K2, SK2P, K2, YO, K1, P1; rep from * across.

Rows 5 and 7: *K1, P9; rep from * to last st, K1.

Row 6: P1, *K2, YO, K1, SK2P, K1, YO, K2, P1; rep from * across.

Row 8: P1, *K3, YO, SK2P, YO, K3, P1; rep from * across.

Scarf

Cast on 35 sts.

Beginning with a wrong side row, knit 2 rows in Garter Stitch (knit every row).

Keeping first and last 2 sts in Garter Stitch for side borders, repeat Rows 1 to 8 of Lace Pattern until piece measures 60" from beginning, ending with Row 8.

Knit 2 rows in Garter Stitch.

Bind off; weave in ends. If necessary, block to finished measurements.

KEY	
☐	Knit on right side, Purl on wrong side
▣	Purl on right side, Knit on wrong side
○	yarn over
⋌	slip 1, K2tog, PSSO (SK2P)

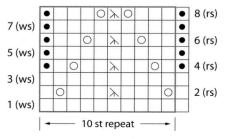

← 10 st repeat →

Lacy Hat

Fine threads and thin needles are not always necessary to create a lovely piece of lace. Behold! A lace pattern becomes a fashionable and warm hat!

SKILL LEVEL

Intermediate ▨▨▨▢

SIZE

Approx. 17 ½" (44.5 cm) in diameter

MATERIALS

Worsted weight yarn

[100% Acrylic, 5 ounces, 251 yards (142 grams, 230 meters)] per skein

>   1 ball grey (A)

>   1 ball ivory (B)

Note: *Photographed model made with Lion Brand®
Heartland #136-149 Great Smoky Mountains(A)
and #136-098 Acadia (B)*

Size 9 (5.5 mm) knitting needles

Large-eye yarn needle

Pompom (optional)

GAUGE

15 sts = 4" (over K2, P2 rib)

STITCH GUIDE

SSK (slip, slip, knit): Slip next two stitches as if to knit, one at a time, to right-hand needle. Insert tip of left-hand needle into fronts of these sts from left to right. Knit them together through back loop: 1 stitch decreased.

SK2P (sl 1, K2tog, PSSO): Slip one stitch as if to knit, knit 2 stitches together, pass the slipped stitch over: 2 stitches decreased.

M1 (Make 1): Lift the horizontal strand lying between the needles; place it onto left needle, and knit new stitch through back loop: 1 stitch increased.

INSTRUCTIONS

Note: *Hat is worked flat and then seamed.*

Rib Trim

With A, cast on 66 sts.

Row 1 (right side): K2; *P2, K2; rep from * to end of row.

Row 2: Knit the knit sts and purl the purl stitches.

Rep Rows 1 and 2 until the Trim measures about 1 ½" (3.8 cm), ending by working a right side row. Cut A, leaving a long enough end to weave in.

Body

Attach B

Row 1 (wrong side): With B, P32, P2tog, P32: 65 sts .

Row 2 (right side): K2, *K1, YO, SSK, K1, K2tog, YO; rep from * to last 3 sts, K3.

Row 3 and all following wrong side rows: Purl across.

Row 4: K4, *YO, K3; rep from * to last st, K1: 85 sts.

Row 6: K2, K2tog, *YO, SSK, K1, K2tog, YO, SK2P; rep from * to last 9 sts, YO, SSK, K1, K2tog, YO, SSK, K2 : 65 sts.

Row 8: K2, *K1, K2tog, YO, K1, YO, SSK; rep from * to last 3 sts, K3: 65 sts.

Row 10: Rep Row 4.

Row 12: K2, *K1, K2tog, YO, SK2P, YO, SSK; rep from * to last 3 sts, k3: 65 sts.

Rows 13 through 48: Rep Rows 1 through 12 three more times.

Row 49: P33, M1, P32: 66 sts.

Crown (Top of Hat)

Row 50 (right side): K2tog across: 33 sts.

Row 51: *P2tog; rep across from * to last st, P1: 17 sts.

Row 52: *K2tog; rep across from * to last st, K1: 9 sts.

Row 53: *P2tog; rep across from * to last st, P1: 5 sts. Cut yarn, leaving a long yarn tail.

Draw yarn tail through rem sts, pull to gather and sew sides to make Hat.
If desired, make Pompom and tie to top of Hat. Weave in ends.

Pompom

From cardboard, cut two circles ½" larger in diameter than desired size of pompom. In center of each circle, cut or punch a ½" hole. Hold the two circles together and thread two long strands of yarn into a yarn needle. Going from outer edge to center of circles, wrap yarn around circles until they are full, adding new yarn as needed. With sharp scissors, cut yarn around outer edge of circles. Cut a piece of yarn 6" long and insert between circles, draw up tightly and knot. Remove cardboard circles, rub pompon in your palms to fluff, trim to desired size.

Lovely Lace Scarf

You don't need a fine yarn to make a lacy pattern. Here's a lace pattern in a bulky yarn: a great way to introduce a knitter to lace knitting.

SKILL LEVEL

Easy ▆▆▢▢

SIZE

Approx. 6 ½" x 44" (16.51 cm x 111.76 cm)

MATERIALS

Bulky weight yarn **5** Bulky

[87% acrylic, 12% wool, 1% other fibers, 3.5 ounces, 187 yards (100 grams, 171 meters)] per skein

    1 ball purple

Note: *Photographed model made with Red Heart® Boutique™ Changes™ #9560 Amethyst*

Size 10 (6 mm) knitting needles (or size required for gauge)

Yarn needle

GAUGE

16 sts = 4" (10 cm)

INSTRUCTIONS

CO 26 sts.

Knit 1 row.

Row 1: K2; *(K2tog) twice, (YO, K1) 3 times, YO, (K2tog) twice; rep from * once, K2.

Row 2: K2, purl to last 2 sts, K2.

Row 3: Knit.

Row 4: Knit.

Rep Rows 1 through 4 until piece measures 44", ending with Row 1.

Knit 1 row.

BO. Weave in ends.

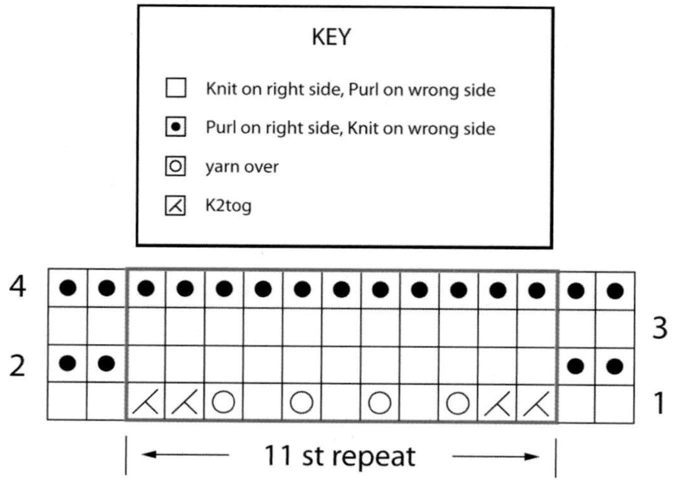

KEY

☐	Knit on right side, Purl on wrong side
⊡	Purl on right side, Knit on wrong side
⊙	yarn over
⧄	K2tog

← 11 st repeat →

Delightful Doily

Easy to make, this is sure to show your friends your great skills in knitting lace.

SKILL LEVEL

Easy ▰▰▱▱

SIZE

Approx. 9" (22.86 cm) diameter

MATERIALS

Size 10 crochet thread

[100% cotton, 400 yards (365 meters)] per ball

    1 ball white

Note: *Photographed model made with Aunt Lydia's®*

Classic Crochet Thread, size 10 #210 Antique White

Four Size 1 (2.25 mm) double point knitting needles (or size required for gauge)

16" Size 1 (2.25 mm) circular knitting needle (or size required for gauge)

Stitch markers

Note: *Begin doily with double-point needles and switch to circular needle when the number of stitches increases.*

Gauge

18 sts = 2" in circular St st (knit each row)

STITCH GUIDE

YRN (yarn around needle): A yarn over before a purl stitch.

Make 5 (M5): In same stitch, work (K1, P1) twice, K1: M5 made.

INSTRUCTIONS

Note: *Mark the start of each rnd with a marker.*

Cast on 9 sts onto one double-point needle. Divide the sts onto three needles; join, being careful not to twist sts.

Rnds 1 and 2: Knit.

Rnd 3: *YO, K1; rep from * around: 18 sts.

Rnds 4 through 6: Knit.

Rnd 7: Rep Rnd 3: 36 sts.

Rnds 8 through 10: Knit.

Rnd 11: K1; *YO, K1, YO, K3; rep from * around, ending last rep with K2: 54 sts.

Rnds 12 through 14: Knit.

Rnd 15: P1: *(YO, K1) 3 times, YRN, P3; rep from * around, ending last rep with P2: 90 sts.

Rnds 16 through 18: Knit.

Rnd 19: *P1, P2tog, (YO, K1) 3 times, YRN, (P2tog) twice; rep from * around: 99 sts.

Rnds 20 through 22: Knit.

Rnd 23: *(P2tog) twice, (YO, K1) 3 times; YRN, (P2tog) twice; rep from * around: 99 sts.

Rnds 24 through 26: Knit.

Rnd 27: Rep Rnd 23.

Rnds 28 through 30: Knit.

Rnd 31: Rep Rnd 23.

Rnds 32 through 34: Knit.

Rnd 35: *P2tog, P1, (YO, K1) 5 times, YRN, P1, P2tog; rep from * around: 135 sts.

Rnds 36 through 38: Knit.

Rnd 39: *P2, (YO, K1) 11 times, YRN, P2; rep from * around: 243 sts.

Rnds 40 through 42: Knit .

Rnd 43 (edging): K1; *K2tog, YO, K2tog; **Turn**, P1, M5, P1, sl 1,**Turn**; BO 7 sts (one st remains on right needle); rep from * around to last 2 sts on left needle, K1, YO, K1; **Turn**; P1, M5, P1, sl 1; **Turn**, BO rem sts.

Finishing

Weave in all ends. Carefully block doily.

Lovely Lace Collar Two Ways

Designed by Lorna Miser for Red Heart®

Wear this collar with the button in front, or button in the back for another look.

SKILL LEVEL

Intermediate ■ ■ ■ ▢

SIZE

Approx. 19" (48 cm) long

MATERIALS

Size 3 crochet thread Super Fine

[100% Mercerized cotton, 150 yards (147 meters)] per ball

    1 ball brown (A)

    1 ball blue (B)

Note: *Photographed model made with Aunt Lydia's® Fashion Crochet Thread, size 3 #365 Coffee (A) and #805 Blue Hawaii (B)*

Size 2 (2.75 mm) knitting needles (or size required for gauge)

Size 2 (2.25) steel crochet hook (for making button loop)

1 small button

55 small beads

Yarn needle

GAUGE

22 sts = 4" in stockinette (knit 1 row, purl 1 row)

STITCH GUIDE

SSK (slip, slip, knit): Slip next two stitches as if to knit, one at a time, to right-hand needle. Insert tip of left-hand needle into fronts of these sts from left to right. Knit them together through back loop: 1 stitch decreased.

INSTRUCTIONS

Neckband

With A, cast on 117 sts. Leave long tail for button loop.

Row 1 (wrong side): Purl across.

Row 2 (right side): Knit across.

Rows 3 and 4: Rep Rows 1 and 2.

Rows 5 : Rep Row 1.

Row 6 (turning row; right side): K1; *YO, K2tog; rep from * across.

Rows 7 through 11: Rep Rows 1 through 5.

Row 12 (joining row; right side): Fold band along turning row with wrong sides together. *Carefully pick up 1 st from cast on and knit it together with next st on needle; rep from * across. Cut A. Do not turn.

Lace
Slide work back to right end of needle, ready to begin another right side row. Join B.

Row 1 (right side): K3, *knit into front and back of next st, K2; rep from * across: 155 sts

Row 2 and all wrong side rows: K6, purl to last 6 sts, K6.

Row 3: K6, *K5, YO, K4, SSK; rep from * across to last 6 sts, K6.

Row 5: K6, *K2tog, K3, YO, K1, YO, K3, SSK; rep from * across to last 6 sts, K6.

Row 7: K6, *K2tog, K2, YO, K1, YO, SSK, YO, K2, SSK; repeat from * across to last 6 sts, K6.

Row 9: K6, *K2tog, (K1, YO) twice, (SSK, YO) twice, K1, SSK; rep from * across to last 6 sts, K6.

Row 11: K6, *K2tog,YO, K1,(YO, SSK) 4 times; rep from * across to last 6 sts, K6.

Row 12: K6, purl to last 6 sts, K6. Cut B.

Edging
Join A. Knit 1 row.

Cut yarn about 4 yards long. Thread beads on yarn.

Bind off 1 st, *slide a bead up to needles, bind off 3 sts; rep from * across row to last bead, slide up a bead, bind off last st. Fasten off.

Closure

With crochet hook, make short chain with cast on tail at neckband for button loop. Join to neckband, secure and weave in ends. Sew button to other end of neckband.

Weave in ends. Block and starch.

Fir Cone Lace

Designed by Scarlet Taylor for Red Heart®

The lace pattern, used to make this scarf, takes its inspiration from the cone of a fir tree.

SKILL LEVEL
Intermediate ▣▣▣▢

SIZE
5" x 50" (12.7 cm x 127 cm)

MATERIALS
Size 10 crochet thread **⓪** Lace

[100% Viscose from Bamboo, 300 yards (276 meters)] per ball

     2 balls pink

Note: *Photographed model made with Aunt Lydia's®*
Bamboo Crochet Thread, size 10 #0705 Pure Pink

Size 2 (2.75 mm) knitting needles

Stitch holder

Tapestry needle

GAUGE
40 sts = 4" (10 cm) in pattern stitch

STITCH GUIDE
SK2P (sl 1, K2tog, PSSO): Slip 1 stitch as if to knit to right hand needle, knit next two stitches together, pass slip stitch over the knit stitch: 2 stitches decreased.

SSK (slip, slip, knit): Slip next two stitches as if to knit, one at a time, to right-hand needle. Insert tip of left-hand needle into fronts of these sts from left to right. Knit them together through back loop: 1 stitch decreased.

INSTRUCTIONS
Note: *Because this pattern creates a fabric that is scalloped only at the cast on edge, the scarf is made in two pieces, then joined to allow for scalloped edges on both ends.*

Lace Pattern (multiple of 10 sts + 1)
Row 1 and all wrong side rows: Purl across.

Rows 2, 4, 6 and 8: K1, *YO, K3, SK2P, K3, YO, K1; rep from * across.

Rows 10, 12, 14 and 16: K2tog, *K3, YO, K1, YO, K3, SK2P; rep from * across, ending last rep with K3, YO, K1, YO, K3, SSK.

Rep Rows 1 through 16 for pattern.

Scarf Pattern
First Half
Cast on 49 sts.

Work in Garter Stitch (knit each row) for 4 rows, ending with a right side row.

Next Row: K4, work Row 1 of Lace Pattern across row to last 4 sts.

Keeping first and last sts in Garter Stitch and center stitches in Lace Pattern, rep Rows 1 through 16 until piece measures 25" from beginning, ending with Row 8 of pattern; place stitches on a holder.

Second Half
Work same as for first half of scarf until piece measures 25 ½", ending with Row 16 of pattern.

Instructions continue on page 38.

Finishing

Place first half on a knitting needle. Thread tapestry needle with long length of yarn.

Hold the two knitting needles in the left hand with wrong sides together. Keeping the yarn needle and yarn under the points of the knitting needles, graft the stitches together as follows:

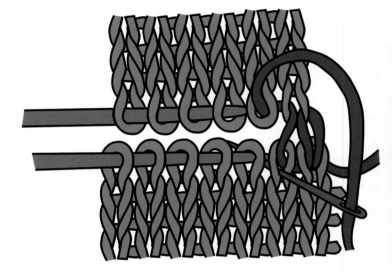

1. *Insert the yarn needle through the first stitch of the front needle as if to knit and slip the stitch off.
2. Insert the needle through the second stitch of the front needle as if to purl but leave the stitch on the needle.
3. Insert the yarn through the first stitch on the back needle as if to purl and slip the stitch off.
4. Insert the yarn through the second stitch on the back needle as if to knit, but leave the stitch on the needle. Rep from * until all of the stitches are joined. Be especially careful to draw the yarn up so that the gauge of grafting equals the gauge of knitting. Fasten off and weave in the ends on the wrong side.

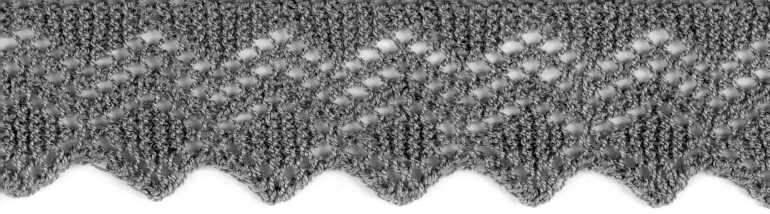

Easy Edging

A simple edging is a great way to practice your new skill.

SKILL LEVEL

Easy ⬤⬛☐☐

SIZE

Approx. 4" (10 cm) wide x desired length

MATERIALS

Size 5 crochet thread ⓵ Super Fine

[100% acrylic, 371 yards (339 meters)] per ball

    1 ball grey

Note: *Photographed model made with Bernat®*
Handicrafter® Crochet Thread, Size 5 #31046
Misty Grey

Size 1 (2.25mm) knitting needles (or size required for
    gauge)

GAUGE

28 sts = 4" (10 cm)

INSTRUCTIONS

CO 24 sts. Knit 1 row; purl 1 row for foundation.

Row 1 (right side): (K3, YO, K2tog) twice, K5, (YO,
K2tog) twice, K1, P1, K2tog, K1: 23 sts.

Row 2 and all even rows: YO, K2tog, knit across to last
3 sts, YO, K2 tog, K1: 23 sts.

Row 3: (K3, YO, K2 tog) twice; K3, K2tog, (YO, K2tog)
twice; (K1, YO) twice, K2: 24 sts.

Row 5: (K3, YO, K2tog) twice, K2, K2tog, (YO, K2tog)
twice, K1, YO, K3, YO, K2: 25 sts.

Row 7: (K3, YO, K2tog) twice, K1, K2tog, (YO, K2tog)
twice, K1, YO, K5, YO, K2: 26 sts.

Row 9: (K3, YO, K2tog) twice, K2tog, (YO, K2tog) twice ,
K1, YO, K7, YO, K2: 27 sts.

Row 11: (K3, YO, K2tog) twice K2, (YO, K2tog) twice, K1,
YO, K2tog, K3, K2tog, YO, K2tog, K1: 26 sts.

Row 13: (K3, YO, K2tog) twice, K3, (YO, K2tog) twice, K1,
YO, K2tog, K1, K2tog, YO, K2tog, K1: 25 sts.

Row 15: (K3, YO, K2tog) twice, K4, (YO, K2tog) twice, K1,
YO, sl 1, K2tog, PSSO, YO, K2tog, K1: 24 sts.

Row 16: Rep Row 2.

Repeat these 16 rows for pattern until desired length.

BO sts evenly across. Weave in ends.

Lacy Market Bag

Designed by Kristin Omdahl for Red Heart®

How delightful to head off to the market with a knitted shopping bag!
What a wonderful gift idea and a great way to encourage ecology.

SKILL LEVEL

Intermediate ▭▭▭▯

SIZE

Approx. 16" wide x 14" long (41 cm x 36 cm) not including handle

MATERIALS

Fine Yarn

[100% acrylic, 3.5 ounces, 307 yards (100 grams, 281 meters)] per skein

    I skein green

Note: *Photographed model made with Red Heart® Luster Sheen® #620 Lime*

29" Size 8 (5 mm) circular knitting needle (or size required for gauge)

Yarn needle

GAUGE

5 pattern repeats = 4" (10 cm)
20 rows = 2 ½" (6 cm)

INSTRUCTIONS

Straps (make 2)

Cast on 60 sts. Knit 4 rows. Bind off.

Top Band

Rnd 1: Pick up and knit 6 sts along narrow side edge of one strap, cast on 24 sts, pick up and knit 6 sts along opposite narrow side edge of strap, cast on 24 sts, pick up and knit 6 sts along narrow side edge of 2nd strap, cast on 24 sts, pick up and knit 6 sts along opposite narrow side edge of same strap, cast on 24 sts. Join in the round, being careful not to twist the sts: 120 sts.

Rnd 2: Purl.

Rnd 3: Knit.

Rnd 4: Purl.

Rnd 5: Knit.

Rnd 6: Purl.

Rnd 7: Knit.

Body

Rnd 1: *K3, YO, sl 2, K1, PSSO, YO; rep from * around.

Rnd 2: Knit.

Rnd 3: *YO, sl 2, K1, PSSO, YO, K3; rep from * around.

Rnd 4: Knit.

Rnds 5 through 76: Repeat Rnds 1 through 4 eighteen more times.

Rnd 77: *Sl 2, K1, PSSO, YO, sl 2, K1, PSSO, YO; rep from * around: 80 sts.

Rnd 78: Knit.

Instructions continue on page 42.

Rnd 79: *YO, sl 2, K1, PSSO, YO, K1; rep from * around.

Rnd 80: Knit.

Rnd 81: *YO, K1, YO, sl 2, K1, PSSO; rep from * around.

Rnds 82 through 97: Rep Rnds 78 through 81 four more times.

Rnd 98: K2tog around: 40 sts.

Rnd 99: Knit.

Rnd 100: K2tog around: 20 sts.

Rnd 101: Knit.

Rnd 102: K2tog around: 10 sts.

Cut yarn, leaving a long tail. Weave through remaining sts, pull tight and secure. Weave in ends.

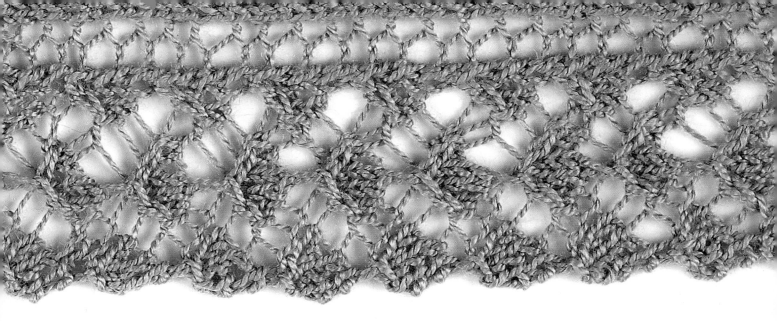

Elegant Edging

Add a lovely lace knit edging to a simple garment, and you've turned it into a masterpiece.

SKILL LEVEL

Easy ■■□□

SIZE

Approx. 2" (5.08 cm) x desired length

MATERIALS

Size 5 crochet thread **1** Super Fine

[100% acrylic, 371 yards (339 meters)] per ball

1 ball grey

Note: *Photographed model made with Bernat®
Handicrafter® Crochet Thread, Size 5 #31046
Misty Grey*

Size 1 (2.25mm) knitting needles (or size required for
gauge)

GAUGE

28 sts = 4" (10 cm)

STITCH GUIDE

SKPO: Slip 1, knit 1, pass the slipped stitch over the
knit stitch.

INSTRUCTIONS

Cast on 13 sts and purl 1 row for foundation.

Row 1: Sl 1, K2, *(YO, SKPO, K1) twice, K2tog, YO, K2 :13 sts.

Row 2: Sl 1 knitwise, P2, YO, sl 1 purlwise, P2tog, PSSO,
YO, P4, YO, P2tog, K1: 13 sts.

Row 3: Sl 1 knitwise, K2, YO, SKPO, K3, YO, K1, YO, K4:
15 sts.

Row 4: Sl 1 knitwise, (P3, YO) twice, P2tog, P3, YO,
P2tog, K1: 16 sts.

Row 5: Sl 1 knitwise, K2, YO, SKPO, K2tog ,YO, K5, YO, K4:
17 sts.

Row 6: (P2tog) twice, then pass first st on right needle
over 2nd st, YO, P2tog, P3, P2tog tbl, YO, P2tog, P1, YO,
P2tog, K1: 13 sts.

Repeat these 6 rows for pattern until desired length. BO
sts evenly across. Weave in ends.

Winter Lace Afghan

Who says you have to limit your lace making to fine threads and thin needles? Why not extend your lace-making skills and make an afghan!

SKILL LEVEL

Easy

SIZE

Approx. 46" x 54" (117 cm x 137 cm)

MATERIALS

Super bulky weight yarn

[80% acrylic, 20% wool, 6 ounces, 106 yards (170 grams, 97 meters)] per skein

    8 balls off white

Note: *Photographed model made with Lion Brand® Wool-Ease® Thick & Quick® #099 Fisherman*

29" Size 11 (8mm) circular knitting needle

Large-eye yarn needle

GAUGE

8 sts = 4" (10 cm) in Lace Pattern

13 rows = 4" (10 cm) in Lace Pattern

STITCH GUIDE

SSK (slip, slip, knit): Slip next two stitches as if to knit, one at a time, to right-hand needle. Insert tip of left-hand needle into fronts of these sts from left to right. Knit them together through back loop: 1 stitch decreased.

SK2P (sl 1, K2tog, PSSO): Slip one stitch as if to knit, knit 2 stitches together, pass the slipped stitch over: 2 stitches decreased.

PATTERN STITCHES

Seed Stitch (over odd number of sts)

Row 1: *K1, P1, rep from * across to last st, K1.

Row 2: Knit the purl sts and purl the knit sts.

Rep Row 2 for Seed Stitch pattern.

Lace Pattern (multiple of 12 sts + 1)

Row 1 (right side): K1, *YO, SSK, K7, K2tog, YO, K1; rep from * across.

Row 2 and all wrong side rows: Purl across.

Row 3: K1, *K1,YO, SSK, K5, K2tog, YO, K2; rep from * across.

Row 5: K1, *(YO, SSK) twice, K3, (K2tog, YO) twice, K1; rep from * across.

Row 7: K1, *K1, (YO, SSK) twice, K1, (K2tog, YO) twice, K2; rep from * across.

Row 9: K1, *(YO, SSK) twice, YO, SK2P, YO, (K2tog, YO) twice, K1; rep from * across.

Row 11: K1, *K3, K2tog, YO, K1, YO, SSK, K4; rep from * across.

Row 13: K1, *K2, K2tog, YO, K3, YO, SSK, K3; rep from * across.

Row 15: K1, *K1, (K2tog,YO) twice, K1, (YO, SSK) twice, K2; rep from * across.

Row 17: K1, *(K2tog, YO) twice, K3, (YO, SSK) twice, K1; rep from * across.

Row 19: K1, *(K2tog, YO) twice, K1, (YO, SSK) twice, YO, SK2P, YO; rep from * across to last 12 sts, (K2tog, YO) twice, K1, (YO, SSK) 3 times, K1.

Row 20: Purl across.

INSTRUCTIONS

Note: *Circular needle is used to accommodate large number of stitches. Work back and forth on circular needle as if working on straight needles.*

Cast on 95 stitches.

Rows 1 through 5: Work in Seed Stitch.

Row 6: Work in Seed Stitch as established over first 5 sts; purl to last 5 sts, and work in Seed Stitch to end of the row.

Row 7: Keeping first and last 5 sts in Seed Stitch work Row 1 of Lace Pattern over center 85 sts.

Continue as established, keeping first and last 5 sts in Seed Stitch and working Lace Pattern over center 85 sts, until 8 reps of Rows 1 through 20 of Lace Pattern have been completed.

Work 5 rows in Seed Stitch. Bind off. Weave in ends.

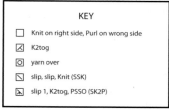

KEY

☐ Knit on right side, Purl on wrong side
◩ K2tog
◯ yarn over
◪ slip, slip, Knit (SSK)
◪ slip 1, K2tog, PSSO (SK2P)

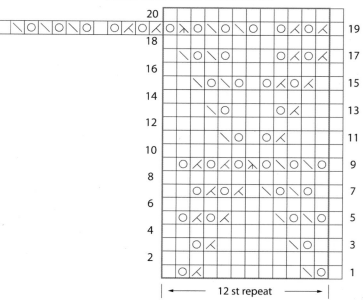

← 12 st repeat →

45

General Directions

Abbreviations and Symbols

Knit patterns are written in a special shorthand, which is used so that instructions don't take up too much space. They sometimes seem confusing, but once you learn them, you'll have no trouble following them.

These are Standard Abbreviations

Approx	approximately
Beg	beginning
BO	bind off
CL	cluster
Cm	centimeter
CO	cast on
Cont	continue
Dec	decrease
Fig	figure
G	gram(s)
Inc	increase(ing)
K	knit
K2tog	knit two stitches together
Lp(s)	loop(s)
Lpst	loop stitch
M1	increase one stitch
M(s)	meter(s)
Mm	millimeter(s)
Oz	ounces
P	purl
P2tog	purl two stitches together
Patt	pattern
PM	place marker
Prev	previous
PSS0	pass the slipped stitch over
Rem	remain (ing)
Rep	repeat(ing)
Rnd(s)	round (s)
RS	right side
Sk	skip
SK2P	sl 1, K2tog, PSSO
Sl	slip
Sl st(s)	slip stitch (es)
Sp(s)	space(s)
SSK	slip, slip, knit
St(s)	stitch(es)
St st	stockinette stitch
Tbl	through back loop
Tog	together
WS	wrong side
Wyib	with yarn in back of needle
Wyif	with yarn in front of needle
YB	yarn in back of needle
Yd(s)	yard (s)
YF	yarn in front of needle
YO	Yarn over the needle
YRN	Yarn around needle

These are Standard Symbols

* An asterisk (or double asterisks**) in a pattern row, indicates a portion of instructions to be used more than once. For instance, "rep from * three times" means that after working the instructions once, you must work them again three times for a total of 4 times in all.

† A dagger (or double daggers ††) indicates that those instructions will be repeated again later in the same row or round.

: The number after a colon tells you the number of stitches you will have when you have completed the row or round.

( ) Parentheses enclose instructions which are to be worked the number of times following the parentheses. For instance, "(Kl , P2) 3 times" means that you knit one stitch and then purl two stitches, three times working 9 sts in all.

Parentheses often set off or clarify a group of stitches to be worked into the same space or stitch.

[ ] Brackets and ( ) parentheses are also used to give you additional information. For instance, "(rem sts are left unworked)"

Terms

Finish off---This means to end your piece by pulling the yarn end through the last loop remaining on the needle. This will prevent the work from unraveling.

Continue in Pattern as Established--This means to follow the pattern stitch as it has been set up, working any increases or decreases in such a way that the pattern remains the same as it was established.

Work even--This means that the work is continued in the pattern as established without increasing or decreasing.

Knitting Needles

Knitting needles in the United States are usually marked with numbers. In most of the rest of the world, knitting needles are indicated with metric. Here is a guide developed by the Craft Yarn Council which shows the differences.

Metric	US	UK
2 mm	0	14
2.25 mm	1	13
2.75 mm	2	12
3 mm	N/A	11
3.25 mm	3	10
3.50 mm	4	N/A
3.75 mm	5	9
4 mm	6	8
4.50 mm	7	7
5 mm	8	6
5.50 mm	9	5
6 mm	10	4
6.50 mm	10.5	3
7 mm	N/A	2
7.50 mm	N/A	1
8 mm	11	0
9 mm	13	00
10 mm	15	000
12.75 mm	17	N/A
15 mm	19	N/A
19 mm	35	N/A
25 mm	50	N/A

Knit Terminology

The patterns in this book have been written using the knitting terminology that is used in the United States. Terms may have different equivalents in other parts of the world

United States	International
Gauge	Tension
Skip	Miss
Yarn over (YO)	Yarn forward (yfwd)
Bind off	Cast off

Skill Levels

Yarn manufacturers, publishers, needle and hook manufacturers have worked together to set up a series of guidelines and symbols to bring uniformity to patterns. Before beginning a project, check to see if your skill level is equal to the one listed for the project.

◼◻◻◻	Beginner	Projects for first-time knitters using basic knit and purl stitches. Minimal shaping.
◼◼◻◻	Easy	Projects using basic stitches, repetitive stitch patterns, simple color changes, and simple shaping and finishing.
◼◼◼◻	Intermediate	Projects using a variety of stitches, such as basic cables and lace, simple intarsia, double pointed needles and knitting in the round needle techniques, mid-level shaping and finishing.
◼◼◼◼	Experienced	Projects using advanced techniques and stitches, such as short rows, fair isle, more intricate intarsia, cables, lace patterns, and numerous color changes.

Standard Yarn Weights

To make it easier for yarn manufacturers, publishers, and designers to prepare consumer-friendly products and for consumers to select the right materials for a project, the following standard yarn weight system has been adopted.

Standard Yarn Weight System
Categories of yarn, gauge, ranges, and recommended needle and hook sizes

Yarn Weight Symbol & Category	0 Lace	1 Super Fine	2 Fine	3 Light	4 Medium	5 Bulky	6 Super Bulky
Type of Yarns in Category	Fingering 10 count crochet	Sock Fingering, Baby	Sport, Baby	DK, Light, Worsted	Worsted, Afghan, Aran	Chunky, Craft, Rug	Bulky, Roving
Knit Gauge Range* in Stockinette Stitch to 4 inches	33-40** sts	27-32 sts	23-26 sts	21-24 sts	16-20 sts	12-15 sts	6-11 sts
Recommended Needle in Metric Size Range	1.5-2.25 mm	2.25-3.25mm	3.25-3.75mm	3.75-4.5mm	4.5-5.5mm	5.5-8mm	8mm and larger
Recommended Needle U.S. Size Range	000-1	1 to 3	3 to 5	5 to 7	7 to 9	9 to 11	11 and larger

* GUIDELINES ONLY: The above reflect the most commonly used gauges and needle or hook sizes for specific yarn categories.
** Lace weight yarns are usually knitted or crocheted on larger needles and hooks to create lacy, openwork patterns. Accordingly, a gauge range is difficult to determine. Always follow the gauge stated in your pattern.